TEN PIECES OF MY FORMER SELF

MEMOIRS OF MY JOURNEY TO GOD

Ivy W. Harrell

authorHOUSE

AuthorHouse™
1663 Liberty Drive
Bloomington, IN 47403
www.authorhouse.com
Phone: 833-262-8899

Published by AuthorHouse 03/17/2021

ISBN: 978-1-6655-1903-8 (sc)
ISBN: 978-1-6655-1902-1 (e)

Library of Congress Control Number: 2021904593

Print information available on the last page.

This book is printed on acid-free paper.

To Jason, Amber, and my grandchildren:

I pray that these stories help your understanding of me.

I will instruct thee and teach thee in the way thou shall go.

I will guide thee with mine eye.

—Psalm 32:8

CONTENTS

ACKNOWLEDGMENTS

My Lord and Savior Jesus Christ: All that I am and ever hope to be, I owe it all to God.

Ossie Harrell and Eva Mae Johnson Harrell, my father and mother: because of you, I am. Though no longer with me, you are always in my heart.

Jason, and Amber: God could not have blessed me with two greater gifts! Despite my failings in your early development, you are my greatest accomplishments, and you blessed me with eight (plus two non-biological) beautiful grandchildren.

Bishop Roy and Dr. Bennie Petitt, my forever spiritual leaders. I got saved under your leadership. Your dedication to God has been inspiring, and your teaching led me to seek God for myself. Bishop: you taught me that without faith, pleasing God would be impossible. Dr. BRP: you were—and still are—there for me, for over thirty years. You will always have my love. You both have left an indelible mark in my life.

Bishop Howard A. Swancy Jr., my pastor of six years. Sir,

your teaching challenges me to go deeper into God's word. Every time I hear you, I look up—because you keep heaven on my mind.

Opal Wright and Hettie Hood, my loving god-moms, I love you. You are God's gifts to me! Always available to give advice, share, listen, laugh, and cry, you epitomize wisdom, style, and grace. You inspire strength, courage, and love at their best!

Former co-workers: I kept your emails from over twenty years. Your encouragement helped me to keep writing!

Specific women's initials of those whom I deeply respect: P. M., Q. J., A. R.-T., R.V.: you all inspire me to no end.

Family and friends: thank you for reading samples of my writing, insight, support, encouragement, and feedback.

Professors, co-mediators, and many others who have inspired me, writers and authors I have read, too many to name here, I thank you all.

PREFACE

My journey shows the consistent power of God delivering and drawing me from a life of waywardness to landing safely in His arms. Having benefited from God's patient grace, I continued to wander. I came to realize in my twenties that I could not do life on my own and that I needed the Lord's guidance. I pray that this memoir will be a part of my family's memories of me. Thankfully, I survived what happened to me, and I now choose to live life to the fullest in the faith that is consistent with the Holy Bible.

Mister Charlie Blues

My father died on December 5, 1998. He was seventy-nine years old. I pause on that date each year and reflect on his influence on my life as well as the brevity of my own life. His world was dominated by alcohol. Whenever I smell stale whiskey and cigarette smoke, I recall one of my earliest childhood memories. It was a time that has always made me feel blurred and dull inside. It was a time when I felt both loved and tolerated at the same time. Daddy said I barely spoke before the age of five and not much after that. Many times, I wondered if seeing him inebriated so much had anything to do with it. Things that defy description: a fragrant flower full of thorns, a stormy night turned tranquil moments later, a raging ocean spray pounding the shoreline to gracefully ebb back to calm in split seconds … that was Daddy. A larger-than-life persona with a heart of ice cream. To this shy girl, he looked and sounded like the baritone James Earl Jones, handsome and booming. But the thing is, he made me nervous when he drank and swore; it seemed like the whole house shook with his rage.

When he drank, Daddy acted out—in Oscar-worthy performances, I might add—by slouching in a feeble posture, like the Stepin Fetchit character from the 1920s, portrayed then as a mumbling, shiftless fool. As though some strange thing had come over him, all of a sudden Dad would slide out of his easy chair in an almost trancelike manner and interject (omitting a bunch of expletives here), "Yas'sar, Mister Charlie … anythang you say, Mister Charlie!" "Mister Charlie" is a term used within the African American community to refer to any imperious white man who conceptualizes all Blacks as lazy, dirty, and dangerous. Consequent to those beliefs, angry bouts of long-felt oppression rose in my dad whenever he resorted to such colorful renditions.

Drinking made Daddy fun at best and scary at worst. I saw that one night when he was in fun mode; I saw that as he zigzagged across the lawn talking to himself. Grandma Chicken, who stayed with us from time to time, picked up a paper-towel-lined Folger's coffee can, spit tobacco through her teeth right in the middle of it as if it were a target, and rolled her disapproving eyes at Daddy as he crawled around on the floor, playfully bucking and neighing, and at me, carefully balanced on his back holding onto his collar as reins—and for dear life, the scary part!—and giving no thought whatever of anything being wrong. Daddy whinnied and threw his arm up, kicked his leg out, yelled, "Ride 'em, cowboy!" The night would end sadly with me trailing behind him with a wet towel to clean up what his insides could no longer contain. In a deep manner, the posture, the renditions, the stupor, my nervousness—all became norms in this young girl's life.

Upon reflection, Dad must have endured some spectacular hangovers following those episodes, yet he reverted to his customary temperament: affably sprawled on his "pallet" to watch the ballgame or to read the newspaper. Many times I wondered if afterward he remembered how his conduct likened to a feral stallion. Or the times he shot off his gun in the front yard after a night of rabble-rousing—it was not even the Fourth of July—he, bellowing fervently, scared the neighbors so badly they called the police. Nevertheless, at a time when many Black men were being locked up for committing lesser crimes, Daddy was fortunate to have found favor with the law. More than once he received a slap on the wrist and was released the next day after a night spent in the drunk tank. Many times I wondered what he had lived through as a child that left him with such scars in his life that he was driven to such a dark side as a man. I never knew, because he never talked about them—ever. Like many Black men who grew up in the Deep South, my father did the best he could with what he had.

A spent life and many reflective years passed before I resolved how Daddy fought to reconstruct the idle-minded discourse allotted to the Black man in the only ways he knew how: as a family man, a devoted father, son, brother, and uncle who came through with help and support when asked. Industrious, he bought and sold properties as well, and before my birth, he had owned a nightclub and played the guitar— or so my cousin Joyce declared. A volunteer, he donated his time at the senior center after he retired. Nonreligious, he had yet a spirit of charity. He praised the value of education and conveyed that no one can take away your learning. A laborer, he worked as a longshoreman for over thirty years and afterwards was elected as Port Authority commissioner. He had only an eighth-grade education, yet at fifty he went back to school to earn a GED to qualify for a promotion to walking boss on his jobsite. A soldier, he was a marksman in the US Army, decorated with medals and citations, and served with the rank of staff sergeant in World War II. Obstinate and with a biting tongue, he never groveled in anything, even when wrongs were done. That devil-may-care attitude of his got him into scrapes with the law, but he never seemed worried about the consequences of his actions.

Those who knew him said that he had a natural gift of exaggeration. He regularly walked around the house whistling and singing, "Old man river, it keeps on rolling along …" or some other negro spiritual. He often engaged in thoughtless habits of crass joking; in my twenties, I tried talking with him about the Lord, but this would get him going even more! So I said less and prayed more. He was imperfect; we all are. He is forgiven; we all are … when we are repentant. I am not regretful when recalling memories of him. He must not be too faulted. At a time when it was unheard of for a Black man, he gained custody of and raised two young children, his three-year-old son and fifteen-month-old daughter (moi), with some help but not much to speak of. Now, instead of becoming a different person when I speak of him, instead of feeling dullness and intolerance, I am smitten with understanding of the someone who defied description. As an adult, I see more clearly how his attributes—albeit shaded by dark coping strategies—led Daddy to the manner of man he had become.

As fate would have it, the apple dropped near the tree. My

own bouts with liquor and sedition that I seemed to inherit did not go unnoticed by those close to me, especially by God. Judgments were cast, and so the story has come and gone. The irony is that my quietness as a child ebbed into a pensive adult who pens my father's peculiarities as the distinctive oddities that they were… that *we* were. But God, refraining in compassion, showed mercy on my itchy-footed wanderlust, a prodigal daughter who came to herself for such a time as this.

As Quiet as It's Kept (First Stepmother)

The physical, verbal, and emotional abuse I received from Anne, my nanny-turned-stepmom, was traumatic, and I was the worse for it when she had an affair on my father. I had taken a bunch of pills the day the ambulance came and whisked me off to the hospital. The sharp sting of the tube being inserted down my throat induced vomiting and made me realize what a stupid thing I had done. But my spirit had collected just about all the damage it could before collapsing and seeing things an eleven-year-old should not have to endure but did. I lay in that hospital bed pondering how I got there. I knew. It was all the *secrets*—secrets I was told not to tell … or else! Anne kept secrets from Daddy. When he divorced my birthmother, he hired Anne to care for my brother, then three years old, and me, fifteen months, while Dad worked. Things worked somehow for several years. Anne kept the house well enough and kept us shining like a new penny. I remember reading books to her: "See Tom run. Run, Tom, run." She was illiterate, and Daddy said he did not know that fact. He married her because she had threatened to leave. "It was hard to find good help," he said. But Anne had secrets of which Daddy was oblivious. One was Tom, her boyfriend, a deacon in the church we went to every Sunday.

This secret if told, I was warned, would get me whooped— not spanked but whooped. A spanking left a bruised bottom. A whooping was different. A whooping was a beating that left the flesh raw for days. The thing is, she would take me with her to her Tom's, not for counsel but for sex. "Stay here and watch TV; we'll be out," he said sheepishly and left me in the living room. I turned up the volume, but I still heard them. I covered my ears, but I could still hear them clearly. I wondered what she saw in him: he looked funny, with a head shaped like an apple ready to rot, core and all, leave off the sweetness of it. He shuffled when he walked and did not have a job that I could see. I would see him perched on the porch whenever I passed on my way to the market.

Anne's beatings were physical and emotional. They hurt worse than bee stings or spider bites and lasted much longer. The times she pressed my hair, which was often, the hot comb singed my ear. When I reacted, a switch landed across my shoulder like she was swatting a fly. "I said don't move!" she'd say. In another instance I rushed home, excited, anticipating praise for my excellent report card. She'd say, "Wha' yo so happy 'bout … yo ain't neva goin 'mount to nuthin' no way!" Although this came from someone illiterate, I understood her clearly. I'd slink away and step inside myself, vowing never to show excitement about anything ever again. My silence cost me dearly. But what else was I supposed to do? I considered running away, but I was young. Where I would go? The fear of *the switch* kept me in plain view well enough. If only I could keep quiet.

Anne took me to church on Sundays. I did so love Sunday school. I learned of God, and I prayed mostly in my head and not so much on my knees. I felt God being ushered into the songs sung by the choir, a presence that seemed always near. I felt that God would be near to the young me, who learned of things much too soon for any child to know. Daddy never went to church. He seemed not to care what any of us thought of that. I called Anne "Momma." because she was the only mother I knew at the time. I felt that a momma's hug should cradle and sweet-talk their little girls. But there was none of that. Instead, there was: "Yo's ignorant, gal!" There was: "Yo's a heifer, gal!" I barely knew those words at the time; however, I knew that they felt like nothing endearing. I believed her, because as a child I believed what my parents said. Two things she spoke of my life's destiny: I will amount to nothing, and I will always be a hussy. Well, there it is, Ivy defined, the gospel according to Anne.

Anne's secrets made me take sides. Taking sides over time ghosted the molding of me as a person, and my young

11

spirit absorbed her words—but not the way a baby is bathed, carefully and caressingly. Rather, her words suggested the way I would imagine a maniacal sort would skin a cat. So, yes, I kept quiet—that is, until the day the ambulance took me to the hospital and my quietness trickled out in ways that changed our whole family dynamics. Perhaps, had Anne kept her disdain of me, the outcome would have been less brutal. Daddy was oblivious about her efforts to hide her liaisons until that day. I know because that day, he hurled a chair at her and dared her to step back into our house again. My auntie drove her to the hospital to get her head stitched up.

Ten years passed before I would see her again. It was at the church where she took me to as a child. My heart desperately wanted healing from her denigrating of me. I barely recognized her; she had aged considerably, with wrinkled demeanor and snow-white hair, once black as a feral alley cat. Her back stooped as she walked with a cane. Surviving on dialysis, I was told. Our eyes met. By God's grace, I feigned civility as thoughts of her halted my innocence. I wanted her to apologize for her ill-treatment of me … an admission of her failure to dote on me as my stepmother. But that did not come. She grinned at me sheepishly, as though she did not really know how to summon a genuine smile. If only her secrets had not stayed with me all those years. If only she had only shown some affection towards me. If only. Perhaps my outlook would be different now. Or, perhaps things happened just the way they were supposed to. She later died of kidney failure, or so I was told.

Now that I am in my sixties, I am suspicious and less trusting of others. And though I have pledged to trust God and to let Him guide my footsteps, forgiving Anne for what she did to me is still a process. God's love compels forgiveness, and I am in God. And if I say that I love God, then I should learn to forgive. God forgave me, thus I, too, must forgive. Forgiveness seems a lifetime proposition at times. But if I do not forgive, how can I move on? Some things take a lifetime to get over.

No More Mas!

M y young mind stayed troubled. The day Daddy and I were in the car on the way to the longshoreman's union hall, where he checked in to see if he can "get out," the term for getting assigned to work at the Port Authority, started out as a typical Friday afternoon. Sitting in silence for a while, I glanced over at him and saw a sparkle in his eyes that I had not seen before. Something was different. I was twelve or thirteen, but his news made me feel much younger. "Baby …" he said, "I'm getting married. Her name is Ada, and she's really nice." His news would change the entire dynamics of our family … again. This time, he was the news bearer, not I. My heart raced. I could barely catch my breath as I recalled a darker time just a few months earlier. Despite a seemingly out-of-body experience I was having, the rest of his words soared over my head like a frisbee too high to catch. How effortlessly the words left his mouth. I remember thinking, I don't care if she's nice, I don't care if she's an angel and could fly! I did *not* want another stepmother ... not now, not ever! How soon he forgot the effects of the last stepmother—let alone nearly landing him in jail! But Daddy didn't remember any of that. Or did he?

Will this wife be like the last one, will she too be nasty to me? Will she show herself one way and be another? There was about to be another stepmother, and there was nothing I could do about it. Ah, but there was. Daddy sat there, a no-filter cigarette dangled from his lips in a life-goes-on-as-usual manner. He had no idea the trouble looming down the road that I was about to cause. No longer a shy young girl, I had evolved into an attitudinal, rebellious teenager. I considered running away ... fleeing to another space, another time, another world. My go-to response to problems was to "give 'em attitude!" My customary revenge tactic was to scrunch up my nose, roll my eyes, and suck my teeth—which I did under my breath, or I'd find myself being slapped into the beginning of next week. At first, my nasty attitude would usually get me what I wanted. This time, it didn't. Dad warned, "If you know what's good for you, you'll work on that attitude!" I snorted, "Humph." A trumpet could have sounded, but I would not have heard it. A bulldozer could have been digging and hauling chunks of boulders right then, but I would not have seen it, for all the attention I paid in that moment.

I paid even less attention to what he said and more attention to forming a rebellious tactic. Despite my attempts at dissuasion and times of wreaking havoc, Dad and his bride married on December 29, 1971, and over the next twenty-seven years I learned that all stepmothers are not alike. The second one was smart. A debutante back in her school days and a licensed day-care teacher, she was "Grandma" to my kids, and to me, she was "Mom." She and Dad took care of each other. They became situated in their mutual easy chairs. They drank and smoked and in the end of their lives became ill and seemed to just will themselves into the grave, too ornery for anyone to help their souls. Dad and his fourth wife stayed married twenty-seven years until his death in 1998; she then followed in death three months later. What an exodus. I asked Dad why he had married so many times. He simply said, "I kept trying until I got it right." Who could argue with that logic?

In the Nick of Time

In the summer 1972 I was fourteen, but experiences had placed me much older. Back home with Daddy and his third wife, I was dead set on rebelling … and boy, did I. I behaved like a zip-dang fool and did all kinds of silly things. I tried things, like getting high off red devils and MD 20/20 and just being fast, as folks would say. Oh, I behaved as though I had caught lightning in a bottle, I was so out there. The term *promiscuous* entered my spirit before I knew what the word meant. One thing that perhaps can be attributed to something mature in me was to ask for permission to get on birth control pills. Dad said if I was going to do those things I may as well protect myself. Young and foolish, my brown body was fodder for whatever man happened to be the flavor of the day. They filled my head with what I wanted to hear. I lived as though I didn't care. I would go off with them and come back spent, emptier than before I had left. I took pills to do away with myself—not enough to die, but enough. I thought no one would notice or care. All the hurt I was feeling, all the disappointments and confusion I was experiencing took a toll, and I was only fourteen. God, please help me.

I was a toddler when my parents divorced, just fifteen months old. Daddy got custody of his two children—my brother and me. The neighborhood I grew up in was middle-class and multicultural: Blacks, Asians, Caucasians, Filipinos, and Mexicans. Afros, T-shirts, jeans, and tennis shoes were all commonplace for us. We jumped rope, climbed trees, played hide-and-go-seek, and skated at the roller rink. I was a child and did childish things. My three closest friends at the time did not judge me. Neither did a few classmates who we hung out with from time to time. We played games at the recreation center, skated at the rink, played in the street. I was in a girl's drum and bell corps—I played the bell and was pretty good too. We were in parades. I was still a child. We caught lizards and rode our bikes up and down in the levee, which later became Interstate 5. My friend's moms did not want their daughters to hang out with me; they did anyway, the three of them. I was labeled as "fast." They were right, but for the wrong reasons. The reasons escaped me also, seeing that I was in survival mode. I started believing that about myself. When you heard something long enough, you start to believe it.

I felt like I was suffocating at home. How exactly does a child bid riddance to an unsavory reputation, especially when it is emulated in the home? Perhaps some children use their God-given sense and do not mimic their parents. But then there are those like me who too easily become what we have been labeled, with all its connotations. Throughout the school years, everyone mixed and intermingled comfortably outside, but inside my house time bombs flared and exploded, over and over. From my earliest memory, I was referred to as being fast, a hussy, and a heifer. I joined others whose hearts hardened from bad relations, unkind words, and unsolicited sexual assaults. Labels are hard to dismantle at an early age— or at any age, I suppose. If a child is being slutty, nothing should prevent caring adults from saying, "Young lady, if you don't respect yourself, no one else will." It still takes a village to raise a child; that has not changed. People may say we live in a different world now, and speaking into a child's life could get you hurt or killed. Speak anyway. Your regard may be added to that child.

Two years passed quickly, and before I knew it I was in the eleventh grade. Without trying, I was on the honor roll. Daddy's voice continuously rolled around in my head: "Get a good education, stay in school!" It was a suggestion that stuck. Going to summer school every year—even though I did not need to—enabled me to graduate months earlier. But that did not stop my defiance, which soared to a new level. I found myself biding my time until I could be out on my own. Anything to escape what felt like a stifling cloak of lead.

Physically, I was there, but my mind was elsewhere. So what did I do with all the hurt and all the childhood angst?

It was a time that would spark a five-year on-again, off-again relationship that became a struggle to hold on to. I definitely was not expecting to encounter what I encountered one day when I was sixteen. At this time, I went to parties and clubs. One in particular I hung out in was the House of 13, a place that allowed in underaged people to do what of-age folks do, and where no respectable sixteen-year-old should have been. Yet God was working. He prepared a blessing just in the nick of time in the form of someone who would become my "hubby" (name withheld for legal reasons). Hubby rode into my life on a 750 Honda. We became a couple the day we met. Aside from a fifteen-year age difference, hubby was a godsend. He brought a balance to my life that had been absent.

One day, just as I was sneaking off with hubby, Daddy walked to the front yard and said, "Don't you think it's about time I meet this guy?" I thought never was too soon for that;

however, I also knew that that was *not* a request. I also knew that Daddy did not really want to meet him and that he probably wanted to douse him with fiery words, enough to make him want to run away and never come back. I could think of a few other places I wanted to be at that moment— like on a shooting star headed towards the heavens; or perhaps in a make-believe place, like one of those cartoon characters my talented sixth-grade classmate, thick-glassed Louie H. drew while swiping his snot-nosed face with the back of his hand every few seconds.

"I'd like to have a few words with you, young man, if you don't mind …" Dad's tone brought me back to reality.

"No problem," hubby responded.

I waited on the motorcycle as they disappeared into the garage. About ten minutes later, hubby came out, and the expression on his face was hard to read. Dad had asked his intentions toward me, and while I don't recall what he said, it must have been a good answer, because we continued to see each other. I was so stubborn that I would have continued to see him even if my father had not allowed it. I think Daddy may have known that. Who knows … who cared?

After graduation in 1975, I was seventeen, and I was offered an opportunity to work as a clerk typist at Lockheed Martin in Sunnyvale. So I moved to East Palo Alto with my aunt Mae and grandmother, Chicken. After six months, I moved back to Stockton because hubby asked me to marry him. We bought a house west of Conway Homes on the south side. I got a job at American Forest Products, where I worked as a typist for two-and-a-half years. We rode with a local motorcycle club. The club of about thirty members rode mostly on weekends. This club did things a bit differently—things like getting along without so much as a cross word between them. And side-splitting laughter and endless poking of fun at other dirt bikers' good-natured expense, boasting of Honda superiority. Hubby presided; I kept the minutes. We rode on poker runs mostly on weekends, to cities both local and long distance. Poker runs are an organized event in which bikers ride along a chalked-out route, called checkpoints.

At each checkpoint, riders receive a small sealed envelope containing a playing card; at the end of the run, riders return to the host clubhouse to reveal the cards. The object was to have the highest poker hand; after cards are revealed, the best hand wins a trophy.

We were true bikers, riding as couples to Vegas, the Grand Canyon, and camping out with the Havasupai Indians, cracking silly jokes at Harley Davidson bikers (aka Honda wannabes). Dark and foggy conditions did not deter us from taking to the highway with our brawny leather vests and bell-bottomed jeans. The house that hubby bought us, though non-descript, was supposed to be where we would build a new life with each other. Our relationship may have been adventurous and fun and the most settled that I had been; however, the fact remains, I was eighteen. Eighteen. Within one year with hubby, I continued to struggle with trust issues—so much so that reciprocating his love for me seemed impossible. He was a good man for me, and to me, by the world's standards. But I was young and lived what I saw in my house. I knew nothing of making a marriage and even less how to flourish in one.

When I turned twenty, we separated, sold the house, and split the equity. He moved to Seattle, and I moved to Los Angeles. We tried to reconcile—but I did not want to live in Seattle, where it rained a lot, and he did not want to live in Los Angeles, just because. Those were our lame excuses. How could I love him when I didn't love myself? When I did not know what love was? Rather than approaching the issue maturely, I ran from him before I got left. He later remarried his third wife and has stayed with her to this day.

I continued to run and didn't know how to stop. Broken, I functioned, but barely. I likened my feelings to Monarchs. *Is that why I like butterflies so much?* They confound understanding. Their DNA is imprinted on their genes. Monarchs move when the sun tells them. It takes months for them to get to their destinations. Despite my feelings, God saw me, a child lost, broken but functioning. He left the ninety and nine and came after the one—not just for myself, but perhaps to use my life as an example to others. I trust in God at all times … "I will pour out my heart to Him for He is my refuge" (Psalm 62:8).

CHAPTER 5

At First Glance

This must be my mother because I look just like her. Though I was not raised by my birthmother, it was hard to watch her waste away right before my eyes. But that is what happened. At sixty-four, my birthmother had two life-threatening diseases: HIV and breast cancer. Either or both could have taken her out. Either or both did. She shunned help. What surprised me most was that she barely kept doctor appointments and refused treatment; she seemed to just accept her fate. Once, I took her to the hospital for treatment, but she was turned away because of drugs in her system. I bought her a meal from Mickey D's and dropped her off at home, and I went back to work. We had our issues, Momma and I, but we were connected. My mind drifted back twenty-five years to my earliest memories of her.

On their way to San Diego Port Authority to see if Daddy could get assigned a job, since work was slow at home in Stockton, Daddy and Ada dropped my brother and I off at Momma's in Los Angeles. He said it was "so we could get to know her." All the houses on her street looked alike, and Blacks were everywhere—vastly different from what my then fourteen-year-old eyes had seen. Daddy would be back in a couple of days to pick us up. I think I should have been prepared for this moment, but I was not. I think Daddy should have talked to me about what I should do when I saw her, but he had not. I had no pictures of her and didn't recall what her voice sounded like.

Daddy and Ada stayed in the car as we—my brother and I—walked up to the front door and knocked; the door opened, and a pregnant girl whom I learned was my eldest sister, Mary, announced our presence. Momma's other children lined up like at a parade, and the main attraction just ambled by. We trailed Mary to the bedroom, where Momma lay in bed nursing a baby. At first glance, I thought, *this must be my mother* because I looked just like her. It was like looking into a mirror twenty-three years in the future. She was a tad darker than I; her brown skin was smooth and wrinkle-free. A thin, multi-colored comforter draped her frame; she glanced over at us and said, "Hi," then looked down at her newborn. Daddy shouted, "I'm gone, be back!" I wanted to go with him. I wanted to walk through the wall and jump into the back seat. Shock, I guess. The days reeled by, and there was a lot of activity in Momma's house: children running around, in and out of the house all day, babies crying. It was all a bit much, but there I was, taking it all in.

The time zoomed by quickly, Daddy came back, and it was time to leave. Once we were home, tension heated up between my stepmother and me. I felt like one of us had to go. I called Momma and begged her to let me come live with her. She hesitated but agreed. One more mouth to feed, I guess. I made promises I would not keep: to watch the younger kids, clean, and, and whatever it took. I had convinced Daddy too, but he was not happy. Eventually he said okay, but not before a speech. "I've been your mother and father! I made sure you had a roof over your head, food to eat. Why you want to go live with yo' Momma, I'll never know!" That was that. Then the final word—"You'll learn!"

Learn, I did. Living at Momma's was a culture shock. At home, I was used to being the only girl, with my own room and my own everything. At Momma's, I had to share a room with my sisters, the twins, who bounced their bodies up and down every night to fall asleep. At dinner, if you didn't get a piece of chicken when it was set down on the table, you could forget about getting a piece of chicken that day. It was June, and school was out for the summer. I wanted to go out skating and to the movies, not in keeping with my promises. Things did not work out at Mommas, to say the least. I was accustomed to doing my own thing. I threw tantrums when I didn't get my way. I discovered that in a house full of children, there was no room for selfishness. After a few weeks at Jordan High school, I wanted to go back home to Stockton. Back to the familiar. Back to chaotic.

CHAPTER 6

SINGLE, MEET SALACIOUS

When I moved to Los Angeles at twenty years old, one of my first experiences left me feeling that I could do life on my own. How adventurous of me, how very bold … or so I thought. I encountered a situation that would leave me literally grasping for my life.

Initially, I had no job and no plan, and no idea what the consequences of that would mean. Single and fearless, I found myself winging it—a lot. For the first year, I slept on my oldest sister's couch. That was nice of her, but I wanted my own place. I soon found an apartment in Inglewood, a small community several miles from Los Angeles International Airport. I had five thousand dollars hubby and I had after selling the house, enough to get by on for a while without having to "live out of a paper sack," as my father would say. I found temporary work as a receptionist at AVW Electronics, a small Black-owned company in Inglewood, and worked there for six months. I then worked as an accounts-receivable clerk for the county for another six months. I was not satisfied. Daddy had always told me to find a job with benefits. So, I kept looking. I figured that I would need a resumé, so as I thumbed through the yellow pages, I selected a company that specialized in resumés.

"Hello, Number One Resumés, Randy Jones speaking; how can I help you?"

I responded that I wanted to speak with someone about having a resumé done.

"How did you hear about us?" I told him. "Well, can you come into the office?"

"No problem."

I shared that I had just moved here and was not too familiar with the city. We arranged to meet in his office in the Wilshire District the same day. Driving in Los Angeles was like being in a maze. Mr. Jones's voice was similar to Billy Dee, and he was chiseled like him too, only taller. He extended his hand. "You didn't have too much trouble finding the place, did you?"

I lied, "Oh, no." *Why did I lie when I really did not have to?*

"Traffic can be kinda hectic at times. Excuse me a minute, okay?" He picked up the receiver, which had rung twice. He crossed his legs and set his feet up on his cherry-wood desk. His eyes still fixed on me, he motioned for me to sit. I eased into an overstuffed, black leather chair. My skirt rose and exposed half my thigh when I crossed my legs, I tugged at it, but it was a wasted effort. Why I felt uncomfortable, I cannot explain. Intuition? I was not tuned into myself enough to know for sure. I was used to attention, but something felt not quite right. I failed to listen to the feeling. The office was decorated nicely.

The song, *Betcha By Golly, Wow* by the Delfonics played from an 8-track system on a cabinet shelf. Oooh, I loved that song! It was turned down low, and I began to fantasize about Mr. Jones there pulling me close to him, slow-dancing, dipping me, and returning me to an upright position after he smudged my lipstick all over his face. *Girl, come back to yourself! I am not here for that!* A small fish tank with about ten medium-sized goldfish swimming aimlessly was situated on another shelf—a smaller version of those seen in Oriental restaurants. A large, well-cared for Ficus sat on the floor next to the cherry-wood desk.

Mr. Jones pointed to a compact refrigerator. "Care for a bottled water?" he asked, as he hung up the phone. I passed, anxious to get on with the business at hand. I was a sinner, yes, but I always believed in God. And I believed that He was with me even when I did not feel His presence—important to know, because that knowledge would be vital in the outcome of this memoir.

"My hobby's trees," Mr. Jones said. "I do resumés for a living, but my love is botany. "Oh, that's nice."

Botany? What's a Black man doing interested in trees?

"Well, now, tell me about your background and work history." He folded his fingers and rested them on the desk.

"That won't take long," I said, and he smiled.

"Okay, give me some background, and I'll fill in the blanks. I'll put something together for you. I guarantee, you'll be pleased." He sounded so sure.

"How much?"

"Forty dollars." Hmm, more than I expected, but I've spent more than that on a pair of shoes, and this was much more important. "You'll have a professionally-done resumé in your beautiful little hands by Friday," he said confidently. It was Tuesday.

"Good!"

Friday rolled around, and he was true to his word. "I can … I'll be more than happy to bring it to you … save you a trip."

"Oh, okay. You have my address." He arrived dressed to impress: silk pants, shirt, tie, the whole nine. "Come on in."

"Okay, don't mind if I do." He had to duck as he entered.

"How tall are you, anyway?"

"Six foot five." We faced each other on the couch. He rambled on about himself, his business, himself. Y-a-w-n.

Trying to keep things general, I asked, "Do you play basketball?"—a natural question considering his height. God, this man was fine. I may have wanted more of him, but my ex, though living in Seattle, was still in the picture somewhat, and I was trying to be faithful. Besides, looking *that* good, he undoubtedly had women everywhere. He didn't say; I just knew.

Mr. Jones, however, had another plan on his mind. "Mmm, girl, you sho' look *good* in those pants!" he spouted, "And you are really wearing them!"

And like a scene that would play just before the movie got scary, I knew what that meant. I smiled half a smile and thought about the last time I wore them. I was seeing an accountant, name unrecalled. We had gone to his sister's house for dinner, and she commented on my pants, said I looked like I had been poured into them.

God, I hope he doesn't think I want to go to bed with him. I mean, it wasn't that I didn't want to, but, uh …, no, not like this, this is not happening. *You've been here before, haven't you, girl, staring down the barrel of lust?* Granted, I am not beyond sleeping with random guys; however, I was trying to do better. Besides, I was still semi-involved with my ex. Again I attempted to change the conversation, but he was not having it. Finally, I politely—but firmly—stood and insisted that it was time for him to go.

Suddenly, he leaped up and very loudly said, "Huh—you ain't gonna tease me and lead me on and not put out!"

"Huh? Wha …—tease you? I didn't! I didn't!" Geez! He must have thought he was so irresistible that no woman in her right mind would say no to him. He paced nervously. I still wondered what had set him off in the first place. Before my eyes he turned from bear to bull, just like that. I eyed my phone and eased toward it, a big mistake. "I'll call the police if you don't leave." *Why did I say that?*

"You'll do *what?*" Without warning, he grabbed my arm

and threw me down on the couch, knelt over me, snatched my princess phone receiver out of my hand, and held it over my head like he was going to smash it in my face. Instantly, my life flashed before me.

"You threatening me? Here's the phone, you want to call the police? Call the police!" Arguing with him at this point seemed not favorable; he was outraged.

Oh my god, another nut! God, please, help me! I was numb and in total disbelief. *What did I do to deserve this? I'm as good as dead. He's going to kill me.* All he had to do was wrap his huge hand around my neck and squeeze until I stopped breathing. *I was a goner. Just do it, just get it over with.* I closed my eyes and waited. A few awkward moments come and went. I made a final attempt: "Will you just please go?" Surprisingly, he stood, straightened himself and, with a look as though we were at the corner getting ice cream, said, "I'll leave, but …" he leaned back on the front door, folded his arms, and even more surprisingly, said, "I want to see you again." He waited for me to say something.

How did he know I was easy prey? In that moment, time stretched like taffy flopping back on itself. Outwardly I was cool and calm. Inwardly, I was a hot mess, and I became annoyed by his assumption that I would want to see him again—men and their expectation that because they look good, we as women gotta give in to their whims. An expectation to *put out* because they spend a few dollars. A cheap date, that's all I was. God, how did I get myself into this situation? I agreed only so he would leave.

"Good," he said. "I'll call you tomorrow." He lowered his head to kiss my cheek and left. Good riddance.

The second he left, I drank brandy, and drank and drank some more, drowning the moment. I didn't care. My life could have been over, just like that, but Randy Jones had stopped short of pulling the plug on my life. It was my fault. I failed to see what that dude was really after.

I called a friend who owned the liquor store and trailer park two blocks away. I asked him to come over right away.

Within minutes, my friend showed up, smelling like a burnt tire; he smoked the most repulsive-smelling cigars.

"Can you put that stank cigar out?"

"Look at what you're wearing!" he said.

"What?"

"Those pants!" *Again* with my pants! Not one to hold his tongue, he said, "Girl, if you farted, it'd take a week for it to smell!"

"Oh, you got jokes. I almost got raped, and you got jokes!"

"*What?* Give me the guy's number ..."

"But what if he comes back and really hurts me?"

"Don't worry; he won't. You'll never hear from him again." I never did.

The lesson I learned is that no matter where I was in life, life's ugliness would come knocking on my door. However, God reached out and held me close. Even when I am hanging on by a thread, I know I can trust God to help me out of situations that lead me astray. All I can do is thank Him for hearing the smallest, most minute prayers.

CHAPTER 7

THE DEVIL WEARS FRAUDA

I had heard about sexual abuse in the Catholic Church. However, I soon became enlightened about how abuse happens in other faith communities as well. If you have not been nearly raped and killed when you were twenty years old and a sinner, you are blessed. When it happened to me, it scared the living daylights out of me, and it scared some of the pleasure of sinning out of me too. After a charlatan masquerading as an ordained minister advanced himself on me, I was left more confused and disheartened about God and lost all interest in spiritual things. I was a hot mess, though I *thought* I was doing well. Drinking, smoking, loose living, all seemed to be easy fixes to me. I was, however, a mere abstraction of myself—and if I am to believe, "Oh, I still have time," then shame on me. Still, I was too deep into survival mode to even take the time to hear God. I distrusted people. No one could tell me anything that I would believe. I marked myself. I rebelled against any and all religion perceived to be helpful to congregants—because in my mind, I had seen firsthand what *helping* does.

Two family members invited me to their Baptist church on Central Avenue. I liked church, and all the good singing and preaching just warmed my heart. I agreed to go. Perhaps, I thought, a good sermon would be just what I needed to deal with my issues. Whatever was preached that day, I do not remember. What I do remember is that I sought counseling with the overseer after the service, which became a disaster. I approached the pastor, and he agreed to meet with me in his office. I was single, no kids, emotionally broken but functioning. In one of what had turned into two hours, I poured out my troubled heart. Initially, the pastor seemed amenable. He said he understood what I was going through. I relaxed in the easy chair, and he sat across from me. He tossed a thick Bible onto my lap and proceeded to recite a litany of scriptures and instructed me to look them up. So far, so good. He picked up a bottle of olive oil, tipped the oil onto his finger and touched my forehead. He held my head as he prayed over me, asking several times, "Do you remember?"—it seemed that he was trying to erase my memories. "Do you remember now?" My mind tried to recall memories; however, it could not. On one hand, I was elated to be free of unpleasant memories; on the other hand, good memories had also left. Then, with his other hand resting on my thigh, he slowly pushed my dress up and began to fondle me. Stunned, I scooted back in the shadowed part of the chair, feeling more lost than I ever had. Every part of this felt wrong. I looked around the room and settled on two pictures on the desk: A picture of a woman snuggled up close to him, a gold band on their ring fingers. The other picture was of two adult children, an adult boy and girl—his, I guessed.

My mind played tricks. What was he doing? He was a family man. Would the girl in the picture speak highly of her reverend charlatan father right now, or would she pout and say a prayer? Would the woman serve him papers, or are the two of them imitators of each other? Are these ponderings even relevant or a nonissue? Admittedly, I had not been to church lately—had things changed this much? Would one have to experience this to understand it? No, I didn't understand it.

Feeling awkward and confused, not knowing what else to say or do, I asked, "So … what about your wife?" The question startled him.

He leaned back, crossed his leg, and said smugly, "Oh, she does what she wants, and I do what I want." His quick response let me know that this was not the first time.

Curious, I asked, "How long have you been married?"

"Twenty-five years."

"That's a long time." It seemed his notion of helping me meant helping himself *to* me. I wondered how often things like this transpired in his office. Futilely, I thought no one would believe me or even care. Especially the mumbo-jumbo part. Especially Momma, with whom I barely had a bond, and who told me that I "must have done something to lead him on."

I might have kept thinking that way if the forces of evil had prevailed. The portrait of a pastor he was not. However, the forces of good hovered, big brother-like. God intervened.

Just then, the pastor pulled me up from the seat to embrace me. And, for the first time in my life, I heard a still, quiet voice saying, "Leave now! Get out!" I did not question it! I gave an excuse and made way to leave. "I have to go now."

"Oh, okay. I have to prepare for night service anyway … Are you coming back?" He grew pathetic by the moment. I didn't know if he meant back for the service or back for him; I did not want to know. I simply nodded.

As he hugged me, I saw his reflection in a floor-length mirror. It looked hideous, distorted, devilish, frightening. "What are you thinking about?" he asked.

"Not much," I lied.

"You're trembling."

My mind continued to reel: *Why me?* Conversely, I felt

hypocritical, like I had brought this on myself. How? Because saying no was problematic. Because, instead of jumping up and leaving the instant his hand touched my thigh, I sat there, curiously mesmerized by his power. Yet, disillusioned: *How could he?* A cleric so easily betrays himself, the one with power. That morning I left home thinking something would be different that day. No clue that this would be it. There must be a special place in hell for people like him. I was embarrassed, humiliated—enough to deter me from being interested in religion from that day forward. I never went back there or anywhere religious. There were no secrets in God, even the secret of a charlatan groping a young woman. He is now a vignette, a fade to black, a blemish, revealed and exposed as a piece in my story. The situation, as egregious as it was, is significant, as I thought it justified my aversion to religion.

I know all church leaders are not charlatans. But there are wolves dressed up in sheep's clothing. God help them. They practice devilish acts and covert hypnosis to deceive the vulnerable. Judge them. Refuse to give them credence. Discredit their misuse of authority. Expose, uncover, and reveal them.

God's timing is impeccable. He revealed Himself to me that day. He showed me that only He can alleviate my confusion. Lord God, thank You for leading me to a place of worship where I do not have to worry about the pastor (or any of the ministers). Lord, thank you for making a way of escape from the pitfalls that I have run into along my journey; and for letting me see you as my deliverer. I am your daughter, and I am okay now.

CHAPTER 8

My Marriages

There is an expression that describes doing something without direction or planning. It is *willy-nilly*. That is how I had lived life up to this point. Doing things haphazardly seemed my modus operandi. Life had taken a toll, and I was only twenty-three years old. The joy of being born again had me feeling like no other experience. I had taken no thought of anything else except to share my good news with my child's father. This news could not wait!

I scooped up my little one excitedly and rushed back across the street. I was thinking, "This is what freedom feels like!" However, on my way home the devil followed me. I opened the door and announced, "I got the Holy Ghost!"

beaming like when I got an A on my report card. Man, oh man, sunshine had nothing on me!

My man dealt with my enthusiasm as a bully creates mayhem. Without acknowledging my good news, the man asked where his shirt was. Not the reaction I'd anticipated. The sweet moment of exhilaration dissipated the way a starved plant withers without water. His insensitivity deflated me, dry and heavy-like. I readied my mind to give him a piece of it—as was my tendency when in fight mode. However, before I could blurt anything out I figured, *what's the use?* My tortured side wanted to kick him to the curb—the nerve of him not being as excited as I was. Staying just ten more seconds next to him drained me.

I stewed for a day, a tendency of mine when things were not working for me. I weighed my current situation, which resulted in my offering an ultimatum: marry me or move out—not quite that cut and dried, but pretty close. I recall a biblical scripture that links living unmarried to sin. I wanted to stop sinning but found it hard. Baby-daddy on the other hand, not one to give in to ultimatums, packed up his things and his two older kids, loaded a U-Haul, and prepared to leave.

However, I guess leaving was not the main thing on his mind, since he came up to me and said, "Let's get married." Not exactly the marriage proposal I expected, and admittedly I should have given the whole marriage thing a second thought; nevertheless, I accepted. Why I accepted was something I have had no clear answer to, up to this day. I could say it was that I had a baby boy; I wanted a family; I wanted ... baby-daddy. So, after my being a member of the congregation for only a few weeks, the pastor and his wife graciously invited us to their home, and on September 19, 1982, we married.

I met James in my mother's kitchen. He had been a friend of hers for many years. She didn't want me to see him. Even then I had a problem listening to other people. It was that *trust* thing again. The attraction between us was instant and mutual. He was my type: handsome, tall, and older—much older. I was twenty-three, and he was thirteen years my senior.

The next seven years of our marriage was tumultuous and spiraling. Neither of us knew what it took to make a marriage work. I was his first; he was my second. To add another element, when both of his sons turned of age, they moved out, but then another son from another relationship was dropped off on our doorstep. I was put into an extra mommy role I was not prepared for. Barely prepared as a first-time mommy, however, I was again winging it without much help. There was no talking on it; I had to make do with what was presented. I took the kids to church weekly. James stayed home or went out with his friends and did not care what any of us thought about that. There we were, sharing a child and another child from a previous relationship, and unequally yoked. I was sad.

My sadness seeped into my daily struggle to be saved and to live a lifestyle that would be pleasing to God. My desire was to go to church as a family. However, my husband had no interest in going. In fact, he only went on Easter and Christmas. Neither did he have any interest in counseling. I prayed for help, for a better marriage, for a better e. Through my sobs, God heard me, though it seemed at first that God was far away.

Two true blessings came from this marriage union, but even they did not keep me from trying to salvage a sinking ship. The first time I left, James convinced me to come back and said he would change; however, things went right back to the way they had been. Every day quarrels escalated into incessant arguing, which fueled my insecurities and his refusal to compromise. Then the arguments circled back to one issue: I did not trust him. I felt he did nothing to nurture my confidence. I left again, but this time I left my children with him until I got situated, with a promise to come back for them. He reneged on giving me our kids. My fear really got the best of me. I suffered and sank near the edge of despair. I started to drink again. I stopped going to church. I numbed my darkness with the devil's tonic. My faith suffered. I dishonored my vows, suspicious that he had too. There was no talking, no communicating. At this point, I did not know what to say. Neither of us did. We hollered at each other, and it even got physical. He became repugnant and hateful toward me.

The devil is real. He used enticing tools to get me to feel empty inside and to give up on my marriage. I felt unworthy of my children. Failure, guilt, and disappointment led me out the door, and the devil followed me. I was sad and miserable. I saw what was happening to me, but I was weak. I was being taken out by an unseen force, and I could not handle it. I missed out on a lot with my kids, and I beat myself up about that. The battle was on. Apparently, battling is not new when couples separate. I was now in that number. My children were being used as a tug of war. They did not deserve that. I recalled having forced him to marry me. I had given him an ultimatum, and he may have resented me for that. He may not have been marriage material—to be fair, neither of us were. Old habits die hard.

After seven years of a turbulent union, the separation and divorce were nasty. Divorce is like a death. If that is true, I had had my share. Nothing was off limits to his prickly attorney, who seemed to relish lighting into me like a barracuda latching onto a goldfish. Like a durian fruit, she was a spitfire mix of turpentine and onion, garnished with a gym sock. Like mulch on a canvas of a sold-out exhibition, she painted me as the worst thing in a pair of jeans. She was not far off. Still, she did not know me, so I knew he was the one that presented those things: the one who had professed his love for me, the one who fathered our children, the one who—himself no haloed angel—contributed as well to the demise of our union. I thought: *Whether those accusations are true or not, don't be a son or a daughter of mine right now; I don't deserve your love or the title, Mom.* Unspeakable acts took me to hell and back. My kids were small, but they saw me. They had hearts. I lapsed into the quicksand of disrepute; I truly was not a good mother to them. Blame me. I do. Give the devil an inch, and he will take much more. Listen to the devil, and he will lead you astray. He will divest you of your shiny repute, strip by strip. You will take on seven more devils when you leave your faith, and you *will* leave if you don't resist. Do not test this part and expect to win; you will lose *everything*. I did. But forgive me now—I do.

Scratch the surfaces of my three marriages, and a blend of recipes for disaster would result: immaturity and betrayal (mine) in the first; suspicion and loneliness in the second; self-will and abandonment in the third; a lack of trust and communication in all. Sadly, my marriages waffled like rubber sticks being pounded into deep mud. Marriage is not something to enter lightly. It has many ups and downs. I cannot say that we—my exes and I—lied to each other, or did we? Or even that we made promises to love forever, or did we, except for those vows? But who remembers those anyway? Certainly not any of the numerous couples in divorce court— certainly not I! My review of marriage was exemplified by the one who raised me, my dad, whose idea of marriage was: "If it don't work, keep at it until you find one that does." I do rejoice in seeing that my children's life partners have been good for them.

I learned late that marriage is not one-sided. It is not Ivy's way or the highway. It is compromise and communication. It is two of the same destiny, something to be determined before commitment to a lifetime together. My marriages became part of the conveyor belt of break-ups, like in *Double Take Fiction,* the drama-filled magazine that shied away from overly melodramatic prose that lacked subtlety and insight. After some growth and maturity, I saw how things might have turned out differently. If only I had followed sage advice, things could have turned out differently. But that was not to be my path. Deep-seated trust issues abounded in me.

Not to be morbid, but I will be gone at some point. None of us will live forever, down here on earth. Nonetheless, I have lived unapologetically in the latter part of my life to make heaven my goal. After years of observation and building courage enough to admit my waywardness, my goal is to preserve what is left of my frame and treat my body as a temple, not to be gamed upon when moods dictate. That is my choice. After experiencing God's goodness as the most wonderful gift ever, it is easier to say no to things I used to shout yes to. It is not an age thing—just nudge the original gangsters still out there who are trying to find their way. Rather, it is a thing where I ask, "Is this all there is?" It is about an immutable life principle that can perhaps be well-argued, but not by me. God wanted me to separate from sin because sin separated me from God.

This journey of mine will stand with others as a testament to the glory of God. It is a calling to honor His shelter in an unsheltered life. The process for me was to realize that real change comes only from God. Real change is to be forgiven and not to continue in sin, but to walk in victory and power in the Holy Spirit.

THE PLANE TRUTH: BLUE YONDER IS FOR THE BIRDS

Since I'm not an avid flier, my first experience on a United Airlines nineteen-seat commuter express is one I shall not soon forget. I felt in need of a mini-vacation and got an idea to get away for a bit, so I booked a flight to Stockton, my hometown. It didn't occur to me when making the reservation that my flight that day would feel equivalent to walking a tightrope one hundred feet in the air without a net.

I should have suspected something was amiss as I approached the check-in counter at LAX, when reality stared me in the face as I viewed the humble set of wings that would embrace me for the flight. I stood there, mouth open, waiting for someone to jump out at any moment shouting,

"Surprise, you're on *Candid Camera*!" When that did not happen, alternate thoughts entered my head about the whole trip. But before I could change my mind, the flight attendant yelled, "All aboard!"

Boarding the small plan did not take much effort. Two steps up a side ladder, a hop, and a simple bow did it. When I got to my seat, I thought a spread analysis seemed appropriate, so I stretched out my arms and almost touched both sides of the inside of the plane. This induced a great deal of reluctance to continue my flight plan, and I was just about ready to dash toward the only door when a woman and her two children in tow hindered me. Undoubtedly she sensed my apprehension because she instinctively began filling in the blanks as I spoke:

"Have you ever flown?"

"This plane is so ..."

"Flown before? Oh, yes, many times," she said. "Small? Yes, but don't worry, it's just as reliable as the bigger ones."

Momentarily pacified, I hung on her every word and established an unspoken bond with her; she became my support system. I felt great admiration for this woman, who was tiny in stature yet had great courage.

Once airborne, I reassured myself, "Okay, I can do this." I tried not to appear nervous, but the sweat on my face gave me away. I shut my eyes and gradually settled down, and for a little while I was in heaven. No sooner had I thought the worst part was over—lift off and being thousands of feet in the air—than we began the descent. From my seat near the back of the plane, I zeroed in on the pilots. They had the nerve to be engaged in a conversation. *Hey! Who is flying this godforsaken, battery-operated crop duster while they are so casually chit-chatting?* That is when I *really* started to pray, *Dear Lord, forgive them, for they know not what they do.* How could they? How dare they? Didn't they know what a bundle of nerves I was? Didn't they care?

I felt doom and gloom and fumed, but no one noticed. Everyone else was either too busy talking among themselves or sleeping. Someone had to be paying attention to what was going on around us—not that I was able to do anything; it wasn't as though I could excuse myself and slip out the back door. *Hmmm.* As we descended, the wind shook the plane wildly; we were totally at nature's mercy. I felt it a good idea to test my new skill since this predicament I found myself in qualified as stressful, so I ticked the boxes: be calm, check; sit in a comfortable position, check; breathe deeply, check; think positive thoughts, check. So much for great ideas.

Finally, I searched people's eyes for courage, dug my knuckles into the seat, and braced for what would come next. *Ahhh*, a perfect landing. After experiencing overwhelming gratitude and feeling a bit embarrassed for having been such a baby, I stepped gratefully and gracefully down from the plane. Suddenly, I was hit by an incredible urge to drop down on my knees and kiss the ground, except at that very moment, I saw someone coming toward me whom I had not seen in nearly three years: my father.

His face beamed, matching mine. I melted into his arms. That moment could have gone on forever, I felt safe, as though

I had never been away from home—until it was time to fly back.

Reflection: Lord God, thank you for an ability to laugh and see humor in things that may seem daunting. Help me to always remember that a joyful heart is like medicine, but a broken spirit dries the bones. (Proverbs 17:22).

CHAPTER 10

MY JOURNEY TO JESUS

The weight of waywardness was gone, replaced by an exuberance too wonderful for words. Three years following the day I surrendered my life to the Lord, the church building where I got saved was demolished and remade into condos. It seemed that the building had been there just for me, and then it was gone. It was uprooted to make room for another purpose, but not before the purpose of my receiving salvation had been served. Much can be said about living a joyful, overcoming life. I know that now because the day I realized that God had me covered was the day my renewed life in Him began. I am so thankful that God did not give up on me. Life has been joyful since my spiritual eyes have been opened. I savor life now in ways I had not before. I look forward with great faith, anticipation, courage, and determination to follow the plan God has for me.

At age twenty-three, on the twelfth day of the eighth month—incidentally, my father's birthday—is when the "tug" began. I call the drawing of God's Spirit a *tug* because that is what it felt like. I remember how I had rebelled against religion because of several so-called leaders I had encountered, who seemed to believe that the way to help people was to help themselves to women in unhealthy ways.

I moved into the La Villa Hermosa apartments on Jefferson Boulevard with my son's father and two of his older sons, the oldest of whom was only five years my junior. They all were off somewhere, and I sat alone in my bedroom, sipping wine and flipping through an *Essence* magazine. As others, I supposed, slept in on a Sunday morning, sweet, melodic music drifted through my upstairs window from a storefront church situated directly across the street. I had noticed it before; however, I was uninclined to visit. Still, I could not help but listen intently; the sound captured my attention.

Just as quickly, though, I crossed my arms and shrugged my shoulders, my "tell" or habit when shunning distasteful thoughts, especially of things holy. I recalled the time I sought help from the pastor of a Baptist church several years earlier (see "The Devil Wears Frauda").

A tug inside of me started it all. Suddenly, I found myself surrendering to the persistent tug—so much so that I quickly showered, dressed, scooped my son up, and strode resolutely across the street to the church. Just as I opened that church door, a myriad of emotions evoked a memory of a specific day that had kept me out all this time—a day when I'd heard God's voice clearly but ignored it because of the pain that ran deep in me.. Yet I imagined God saying, *Let me guard this child before she perishes without Me, kills someone, or ends up in jail!* Being pulled by the invisible tug may have seemed unreal, even enigmatic to some, if a mind wanted to think such things. However, the reality of the moment pinged this as the time to put aside old, yet still fresh, wounds. The time had come when love was to be made indisputable, and hope as a wonder in my soul. I slid into a seat and listened as the preacher preached. I soon felt as though I was where I needed to be. After two more visits to the church across the street, the invitation for anyone who wanted to receive salvation was offered. However, I thought I still was not ready: living unmarried to my son's father; drinking, smoking, and doing whatever else I wanted to do; and … geez, did God even want somebody like me?

I could not resist the tug. Yet, behind the resolve was great trepidation. Nevertheless, I walked down to the altar and accepted the invitation into the kingdom of God. My yes, however, did not include knowing what all was entailed. Was I even supposed to know? Would it mean that I would have to give up my man? Sex? Drinking? Smoking? A word came forth: *Your body is the temple of the Holy Ghost. No longer defile it.* I guess I had my answer. That day, I emerged from the water, baptized in the name of Jesus. Reborn. That night, I returned to tarry (wait) for God to fill me with His Spirit. *What does that even mean?* I wondered. That night, I got on my knees, raised my hands toward heaven, and began to cry out to God with my voice: "Hallelujah! Hallelujah! Hallelujah!" Within a few minutes, something enshrouded me, something that I had never felt before. I heard myself speaking in another language that was unfamiliar to me. It had me feeling elated. I rejoiced as an invisible and indescribable companion received me, this ... this new emergence. It is joyful, it is overcoming, it is victorious. Now, to savor life in ways that I had not before left me with great faith, anticipation, courage, and determination.

While out being buck wild, God was setting me up to experience repentance. The tug meant everything to me that Sunday in September 1982. It meant that God saw me. It meant freedom to me. That day, my heart made me run to Him as one running for her life. I ceased from the things that weakened me and came to trust God for my needs. Since then, I have not wanted or needed for anything. Jesus has taken excellent care of me. Now I can without hesitation share my testimony. Every piece of my life up to this point, no matter how bad things got, held within it a blessing of some kind. And now, with God's help, I can move forward to higher levels in Him. I will always remember what God has done for me. How He has been there through each piece of my story. The desert-like experiences taught me to go deep into God's word for *shade*. Every piece carried me on a journey of reflection, and I learned.

I learned that when things go wrong and the weight of the wrongness wants to consume me, God will make a way of escape for me. I learned that reflection helps in seeing more clearly the poor decisions and thoughtless choices, some I barely lived through. I learned that my past—as unsheltered as it was—does not define me. I submit no regrets only gratefulness to God for having made it through, piece by piece.

ABOUT THE AUTHOR

I vy Harrell was born and raised in Stockton, California, primarily by her father. She moved to Los Angeles, California, around 1980, where she has lived since. She worked for a local aerospace company for thirty-eight years before retiring in November 2019. She enjoys family, gardening, reading, and listening to music.

Ivy is active in church and community. She is a former member of Miracle Center Apostolic Church and currently fellowships at Peace Apostolic Church. Ivy is passionately involved in the Women's Ministry and Missionary Auxiliary. She volunteered at the Institute for Non-Violence in Los Angeles (INVLA) and for the Los Angeles City Attorney's Dispute Resolution Program for over ten years, where she worked with community members and law enforcement officers to promote concepts of neutrality and conciliation in resolving disputes. Ivy has received awards in ethics and volunteerism in public service.

Ivy stepped into various writing genres over her life—short stories, personal essays, personalized poetry, profiles, and vignettes—all of which have given her great satisfaction, and she continues to enjoy living for God and writing.